REAL MONSTERS

KOMODO DRAGON

TOXIC LIZARD TITAN

JILLIAN L. HARVEY

Checkerboard
Library

An Imprint of Abdo Publishing
abdopublishing.com

ABDOPUBLISHING.COM

Published by Abdo Publishing, a division of ABDO, PO Box 398166, Minneapolis, Minnesota 55439. Copyright © 2017 by Abdo Consulting Group, Inc. International copyrights reserved in all countries. No part of this book may be reproduced in any form without written permission from the publisher. Checkerboard Library™ is a trademark and logo of Abdo Publishing.

Printed in the United States of America, North Mankato, Minnesota
092016
012017

Design: Christa Schneider, Mighty Media, Inc.
Production: Mighty Media, Inc.
Editor: Liz Salzmann
Cover Photo: Shutterstock Images
Interior Photos: Alamy, p. 19; AP Images, p. 29; From The New York Public Library, p. 9; Getty Images, p. 27; iStockphoto, p. 25; Mighty Media, Inc., pp. 7, 23; Shutterstock Images, pp. 4, 5, 6, 7, 11, 13, 15, 17, 21

Publisher's Cataloging-in-Publication Data

Names: Harvey, Jillian L., author.
Title: Komodo dragon : toxic lizard titan / by Jillian L. Harvey.
Other titles: Toxic lizard titan
Description: Minneapolis, MN : Abdo Publishing, 2017. | Series: Real monsters |
    Includes bibliographical references and index.
Identifiers: LCCN 2016944833 | ISBN 9781680784213 (lib. bdg.) |
    ISBN 9781680797749 (ebook)
Subjects: LCSH: Komodo dragons--Juvenile literature.
Classification: DDC 597.95--dc23
LC record available at http://lccn.loc.gov/2016944833

CONTENTS

MEET A **KOMODO DRAGON**

AS IT **HUNTS PREY THREE TIMES** ITS SIZE!!!

The sun shines brightly over Komodo Island. A Komodo dragon lurks in the shadows. It catches the scent of a water buffalo several miles away. The giant lizard makes its way to the buffalo. It comes up behind the huge mammal. The dragon sinks its teeth into the buffalo's ankle. Its powerful jaws pull muscle from bone.

The buffalo kicks itself free. It limps away, but blood loss and the dragon's venom start slowly killing the animal. The lizard patiently follows the buffalo. After five days, the giant beast falls dead. It's chow time for the dragon.

CREATURE FEATURE

NAME: Komodo dragon

NICKNAMES: Land crocodile, monitor lizard, goanna

CLASS: Reptilia

SIZE: 6.5 to 10 feet (2 to 3 m) long

WEIGHT: 150 to 350 pounds (68 to 160 kg)

COLORATION: Black, brown, grayish-red, grayish-yellow

LIFE SPAN: Up to 50 years

MONSTROUS CHARACTERISTICS

> Toxic **venom**

> **Serrated**, curved teeth

> Massive, prehistoric-looking body

> Forked tongue

> Sharp claws

MAP KEY Komodo Dragon Range

INDONESIA
(NATION OF ISLANDS)

FLORES
RINCA
KOMODO

GILA MOTANG

INDIAN OCEAN

> Range: Lesser Sunda Islands, Indonesia (Komodo, Rinca, Gila Motang, and Flores)

> Diet: Deer, wild boars, small **rodents**, water buffalo, and even other Komodo dragons

FUN FACT

In 1926, W. Douglas Burden led an expedition to capture Komodo dragons for a museum. This event inspired the classic 1933 movie *King Kong*.

HERE BE DRAGONS

Close your eyes and picture a dragon. Does it look soft and cuddly? Is it playful? Probably not. Dragons are beasts of legend. They have haunted our human imaginations for centuries.

Sailors in the 1500s warned of a monster that plagued their travels in certain foreign lands. The legend of giant reptiles that devoured humans spread fear among the bravest of men for many years. Today, these lands are Indonesia, home of the Komodo dragon.

Although Komodo dragons have a monstrous reputation, not everyone sees them as evil. Local Indonesian **folklore** tells of a woman called the Dragon Princess. The princess gave birth to an egg in a cave. A dragon hatched from the egg and the princess named it Ora. Natives of the islands still believe the Komodo dragon is descended from a princess. They honor the creature with great respect.

The Hunt-Lenox globe was created around 1510. It has "HC SVNT DRACONES" written near present-day Indonesia and Malaysia. This phrase is Latin for "Here be dragons."

It wasn't until 1910 that Europeans discovered that massive lizards actually existed in Indonesia. That year, Dutchman J.K.H. van Steyn van Hensbroek traveled to Indonesia to try and find them. Van Steyn van Hensbroek came across many giant lizards. One was six feet (2 m) long.

Van Steyn van Hensbroek killed the giant reptile. He sent its scaly skin to **naturalist** Peter Ouwens. Ouwens examined the skin and wrote the Komodo dragon's first official scientific **description** in 1912.

Over the next 100 years, Komodo dragons were studied and hunted. In 1926, American scientist W. Douglas Burden led an expedition to the Indonesian islands. He returned to the United States with one live Komodo dragon and twelve that were dead. Two of these lizards are on display in the American Museum of Natural History in New York City, New York. Burden is credited with giving the dragons the common name "Komodo dragon."

We've learned a lot about Komodo dragons through studying them dead and alive. But much about these creatures remains a mystery. As the world's largest living lizards, many still consider the dragons to be frightening creatures.

Today, killing Komodo dragons is illegal. People continue to study these lizards in the animals' natural environment.

A DRAGON'S LIFE

Every year between May and August, life gets a little more exciting on Komodo Island. Komodo dragons usually live alone. But in the summer they come together for mating season. For about three months, blood is spilled on the island by male dragons.

During the mating season, the males prove their strength to the females. They do this by fighting. Often blood is drawn, but these battles are not meant to be a fight to the death. Afterward, the winner will approach the female to mate.

A female dragon lays eggs between July and September. She sometimes digs a hole in a hillside for the eggs. Other times she lays the eggs in an empty bird's nest she has invaded.

A dragon nest, or clutch, can have as many as 30 eggs. The female protects them for up to three months. She may even dig a **decoy** nest to trick predators and prevent them from harming her clutch.

Male Komodo dragons stand on their hind legs and hit each other with their forelimbs and tails.

After about nine months, the dragon eggs hatch. Komodo dragon hatchlings fend for themselves as soon as they are born. Their mother does not care for them. The baby dragons often get killed by predators. In fact, adult dragons may eat the newborn creatures!

For safety, hatchlings quickly climb trees, out of reach of predators roaming the ground. Hatchlings eat only insects at first. As they grow, they add small snakes, birds, and **rodents** to their diet.

After living in the trees for about four years, it is safe for the dragons to come down permanently. They are nearly full grown and no longer need the protection of the trees. The dragons will never return to their high perches, as adults are too heavy to climb trees.

Komodo dragons that survive to adulthood often live long lives. In zoos they live about 25 years. Scientists think these lizards may live up to twice as long in their natural **habitat**!

NO MATING? NO KIDDING!

Komodo dragons are a rare species of animal that can reproduce both sexually and asexually. The females can mate with males. Or, they can also lay eggs all on their own. There have been at least two cases of this type of dragon reproduction. Both females lived in zoos. This type of reproduction results in only male babies.

Dragons grow up to four feet (1.2 m) long during the years they live in trees.

LONELY LIZARDS

Komodo dragons make their home on Indonesia's Lesser Sunda Islands. This string of islands lies in the Flores Sea. There, the dragons live primarily within Komodo National Park. The park is made up of several islands. Sections of the west coast of Flores are part of the park as well.

Existing only on these few islands, the dragons live a life very **isolated** from the rest of the world. This both hurts and helps the dragons. Living in such a small area means that the dragon population is sensitive to change.

For example, if a disease spreads through the islands, all the world's Komodo dragons could be affected. On the other hand, Komodo dragons are at the top of their food chain on the islands. Living in an isolated area that lacks natural predators during their adulthood helps keep the dragon population strong.

Originally, Komodo dragons roamed eastern Australia. They migrated to Indonesia about 900,000 years ago.

ISLAND HABITAT

The **terrain** on the islands where Komodo dragons live varies greatly. There are beaches, mountains, **savannas**, and woodlands. The dragons move throughout all the areas. But they spend most of their time between the wet forests and dry savannas.

Komodo dragons find a lot of prey in the trees and grass of these areas. Additionally, the brown and green of these plants act as camouflage for the dragons. By blending in with their surroundings, dragons are able to patiently lie in wait for prey.

Komodo dragons need a **habitat** with warm temperatures to survive. They are ectotherms, which means they use the sun to warm their bodies. But sometimes dragons need a break from the heat. To cool down, they dig burrows that keep them out of the sun during long, bright days. They use these same burrows to keep warm in the coolness of night.

A Komodo dragon lies still among leaves and rocks. If the water buffalo gets too close, the dragon will attack!

SCALY SCAVENGER

People often think of dragons as loud, savage animals. Attacking prey, after all, can cause quite a commotion. But unlike mythical fire-breathing dragons, Komodo dragons are typically quiet creatures. However, they sometimes will make a low hissing sound.

Outside of mating season, Komodo dragons spend most of their time alone. They are diurnal, which means they sleep at night and are awake during the day. Komodo dragons sleep about 12 hours per night. The rest of their time is spent looking for food.

Komodo dragons are opportunistic carnivores. This means they eat meat and they are not picky. Dragons will hunt prey of all sizes, from **rodents** to water buffaloes. And they will eat **carrion** as well. This makes the Komodo dragon both a predator and a **scavenger**. To search for food, these giant lizards rely on their sense of smell. They smell with their thin, forked tongues.

Komodo dragons constantly flick their tongues, which is how they smell. A dragon can smell prey or carrion up to seven miles (11 km) away.

The way dragons kill their prey is one of the most unusual things about them. For many years it was believed that their **saliva** contained a toxic bacteria. After one bite from a dragon, the bacteria would poison the prey. As the bacteria spread through the victim's body, the dragon would follow the animal, patiently waiting. Eventually the animal would die, and the Komodo dragon would be rewarded with a tasty meal.

In 2009, Australian researcher Bryan Fry discovered that the bacteria theory was wrong. Komodo dragons do not have deadly bacteria in their mouths. They do, however, poison their prey with **venom**.

The dragon's venom causes an animal to go into shock. It also keeps the animal's blood from clotting. So, the prey eventually dies of blood loss from the dragon's bite wound.

A Komodo dragon can eat up to 80 percent of its body weight in one sitting. It usually eats one large animal per month. The rest of the time it eats whatever smaller animals and birds it can find.

EFFICIENT EATERS

Komodo dragons work hard and wait patiently for their food. This effort is not in vain. Many carnivores only eat certain parts of their prey, leaving the rest to rot. But dragons are not so wasteful. They devour nearly all of their prey. This includes the bones, hooves, and hides of the animals.

KOMODO DRAGON: PREDATOR AND PREY

KOMODO DRAGON

DEER

GOAT

WATER BUFFALO

WILD BOAR

SNAKE

EGGS

Adult Komodo dragons have no natural predators. They eat anything they can catch or find already dead. This includes deer, goats, wild boar, water buffalo, and snakes. Komodo dragons will also invade bird and turtle nests to eat the eggs.

VULNERABLE GIANTS

While adult Komodo dragons don't have natural predators, there are other ways they are threatened. Human actions have a huge influence on Komodo dragons. These actions influence the animals both directly and indirectly.

These giant lizards have been hunted as **exotic** animals. Their skin and feet were sought for trading. Hunters **poached** them for **trophies**. And many dragons were captured for zoos.

Today, the Komodo dragon is listed as a **vulnerable** species. But its population is currently stable. This is due mainly to the creation of Komodo National Park in 1980.

The park was created by conservationists. They understood the need for protecting these interesting lizards that give us a glimpse of ancient times. Inside the park, the dragons are generally safe. It is illegal to hunt them, although sometimes this rule is broken.

Nearly 6,000 Komodo dragons live in Komodo National Park. The park was declared a World Heritage Site in 1991.

Unfortunately, **poaching** is not the only threat affecting the dragons' future. As more people come to the islands, the dragons' **habitat** is shrinking. Human farms and agriculture are taking the place of dragons' homes and feeding grounds.

People also hunt the dragons' natural prey, such as deer and pigs. This makes these animals less available to the dragons. This type of hunting caused the disappearance of the dragons on the island of Padar. No dragons have been seen there since 1970.

Another major threat to dragons is their limited range. Remember that the dragons exist in only one spot on Earth. This makes them particularly sensitive to **climate change** and natural disasters in that area.

Rising sea levels caused by **global warming** mean less beach habitat. Forest fires destroy trees. Fewer trees mean the deer have less to eat. This decreases the deer population, meaning the dragons have less food.

FUN FACT
Komodo dragons continue to slowly grow throughout their entire lives.

Sixteen Komodo dragons hatched at the Memphis Zoo in Memphis, Tennessee, in 2013.

GLOSSARY

carrion — dead, rotting animal flesh.

climate change — a long-term change in Earth's climate, or in that of a region of Earth. It includes changing temperatures, weather patterns, and more. It can result from natural processes or human activities.

decoy — an action or object used to attract attention so something else will not be noticed.

description — a written or spoken statement that tells about someone or something.

endangered — in danger of becoming extinct.

exotic — interesting because it is strange or different from the usual.

folklore — the stories, customs, and beliefs of the common people that are handed down from person to person.

global warming — an increase in the temperature of Earth's atmosphere and oceans.

habitat — a place where a living thing is naturally found.

isolated — separated from others.

naturalist — someone who studies plants, animals, and other living things.

poach — to hunt or fish illegally.

WEBSITES

To learn more about Real Monsters, visit **booklinks.abdopublishing.com**. These links are routinely monitored and updated to provide the most current information available.

resilient — able to become strong or healthy again after something bad happens.

rodent — any of several related animals that have large front teeth for gnawing. Common rodents include mice, squirrels, and beavers.

saliva — a liquid produced in the mouth. It keeps the mouth moist and helps in chewing, swallowing, and breaking down food.

savanna — a grassy plain with few or no trees.

scavenger — a person or animal who searches through waste for something that can be used.

serrated — notched like a saw.

terrain — the natural features of an area of land, such as mountains and rivers.

trophy — a game animal or fish suitable to be preserved and displayed.

venom — a poison produced by some animals and insects. It usually enters a victim through a bite or a sting.

vulnerable — able to be hurt or attacked. An animal has a vulnerable status when it is likely to become endangered.

INDEX